Even an Octopus Needs a Home

Irene Kelly

Holiday House / New York

HOLIDAY HOUSE is registered in the U.S. Patent and Trademark Office.
Printed and Bound in May 2011 at Kwong Fat Offset Printing Co., Ltd., Dongguan City, China.
The text typeface is Christine.
The illustrations were done in watercolor, gouache, and pen and ink.
www.holidayhouse.com
First Edition
1 3 5 7 9 10 8 6 4 2

Library of Congress Cataloging-in-Publication Data
Kelly, Irene.
Even an octopus needs a home / by Irene Kelly. — 1st ed.
p. cm.
ISBN 978-0-8234-2235-7 (hardcover)
1. Nests—Juvenile literature. 2. Animals—Habitations—Juvenile literature. I. Title.
QL756.K45 2011
591.56'4—dc22
2010029441

There's no place like home.
That's true for people and animals.
Animals need homes for many of
the same reasons people do.

They need a safe place to sleep,
store food, and raise their families.

How does an animal make its home?
Some animals build with branches;
others sculpt with mud or weave with sticks.
Some simply curl up in a cave or take shelter
in the hollow of a tree.
And for one little spider, all it takes is a bubble. . . .

Tree houses

Chimpanzees love a view. But they want a new one every night. Each evening, chimps make new nests high up in trees. It only takes a few minutes for the chimps to bend branches and build sturdy sleeping platforms as high as eighty feet off the ground. Young chimps have fun jumping up and down on their beds.

Sound familiar?

Monk parakeets create huge treetop apartment buildings.
The construction begins with just one pair of birds.

The two parakeets weave sticks together
to make a ball-shaped nest.
Another pair comes along and
adds its nest to the first one.

Honduran white bats nibble the veins on leaves, causing the leaves to fold. Up to twelve bats can sleep together in one leaf tent.

More and more parakeets add nests to the ever-growing home until a bustling colony has been created. Some monk parakeet nests can be as big as a car!

Bees, wasps, and some ants make themselves at home in trees.

honeycomb

Honeybees begin the big job of building their hives by squeezing tiny bits of wax out of their abdomens.

They chew and mold the wax flakes into cells, which the bees layer to make into a honeycomb.

The honeycomb is a nursery for baby bees (larvae) and a pantry for storing honey.

honey

close-up

larva

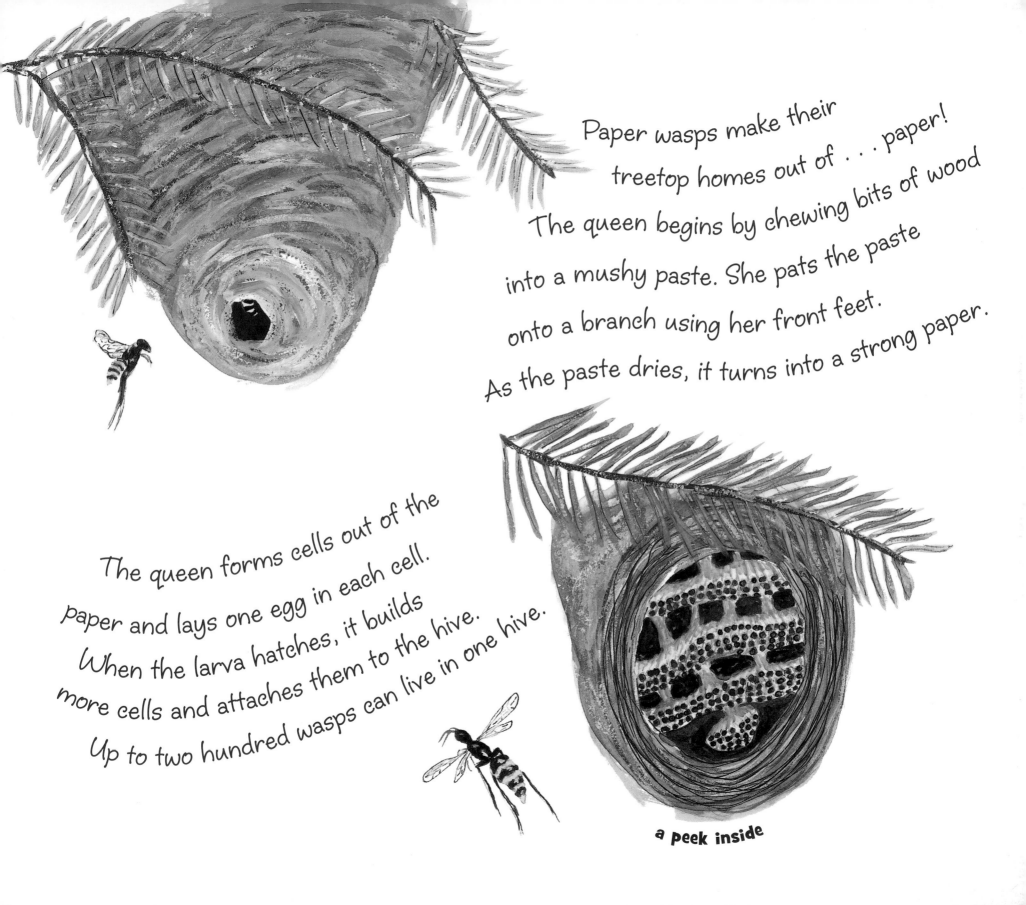

Paper wasps make their treetop homes out of . . . paper! The queen begins by chewing bits of wood into a mushy paste. She pats the paste onto a branch using her front feet. As the paste dries, it turns into a strong paper.

The queen forms cells out of the paper and lays one egg in each cell. When the larva hatches, it builds more cells and attaches them to the hive. Up to two hundred wasps can live in one hive.

a peek inside

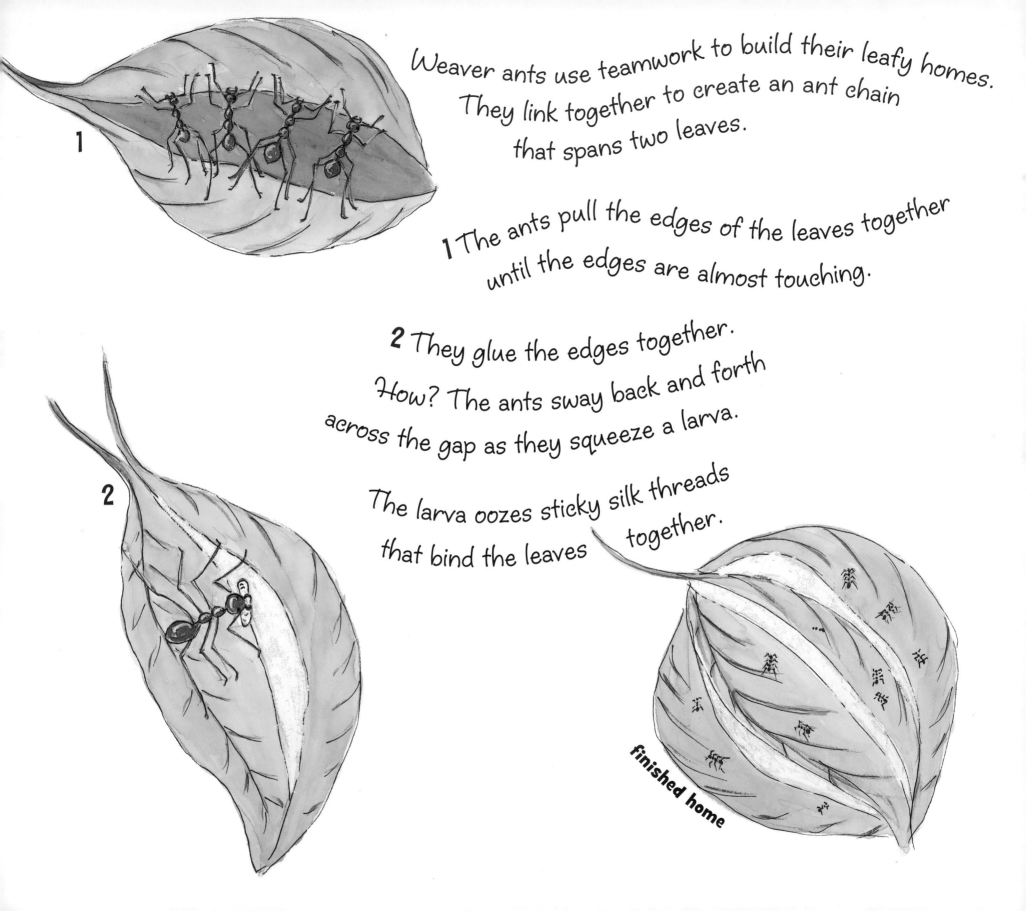

Weaver ants use teamwork to build their leafy homes. They link together to create an ant chain that spans two leaves.

1 The ants pull the edges of the leaves together until the edges are almost touching.

2 They glue the edges together. How? The ants sway back and forth across the gap as they squeeze a larva.

The larva oozes sticky silk threads that bind the leaves together.

finished home

Weaver birds push, pull, and knot fibers and vines to create their woven homes. Female Montezuma Oropendolas make purselike nests that can be six feet long!

These industrious birds live in large groups, or colonies. A single colony usually contains 30 nests, but up to 172 nests have been spotted in one tree!

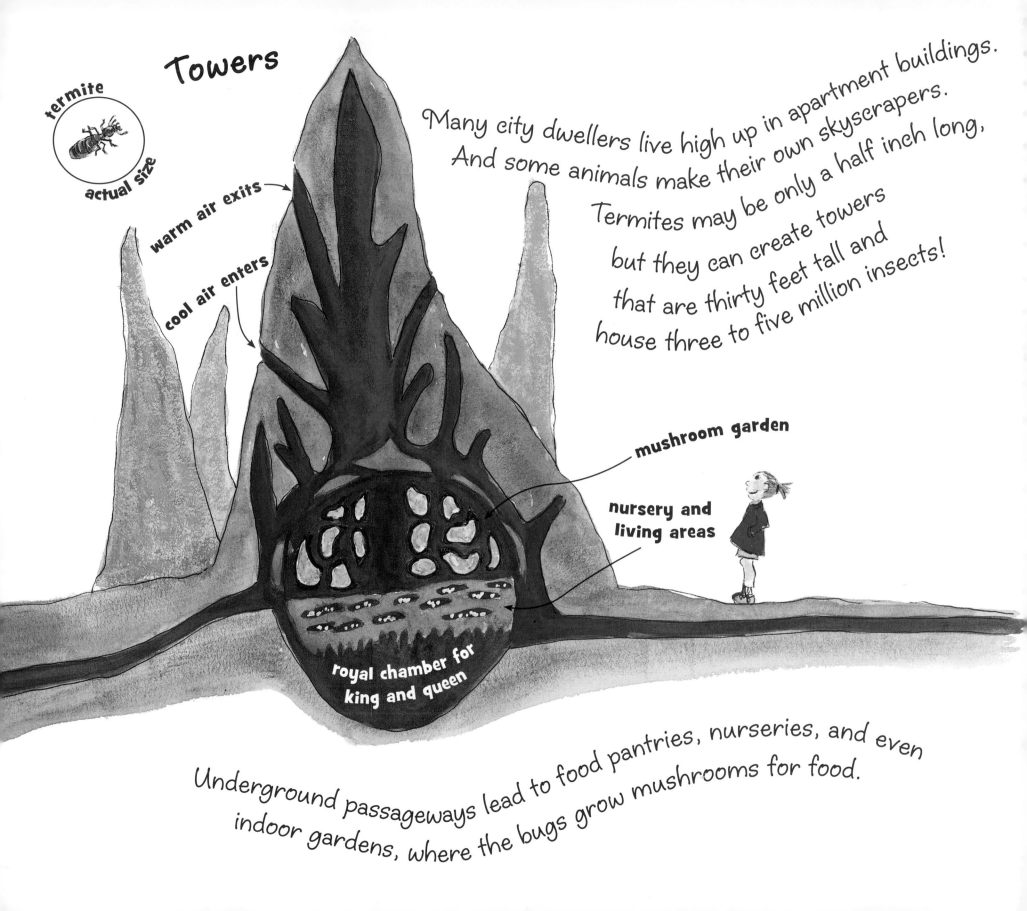

Towers

termite
actual size

warm air exits

cool air enters

Many city dwellers live high up in apartment buildings.
And some animals make their own skyscrapers.
Termites may be only a half inch long,
but they can create towers
that are thirty feet tall and
house three to five million insects!

mushroom garden

nursery and
living areas

royal chamber for
king and queen

Underground passageways lead to food pantries, nurseries, and even
indoor gardens, where the bugs grow mushrooms for food.

European red wood ants build the tallest towers of all ants. They stack pine needles and twigs until they have constructed a mound—up to six feet high. This tower hides and protects a maze of tunnels and chambers underneath, where the ants live and raise their young.

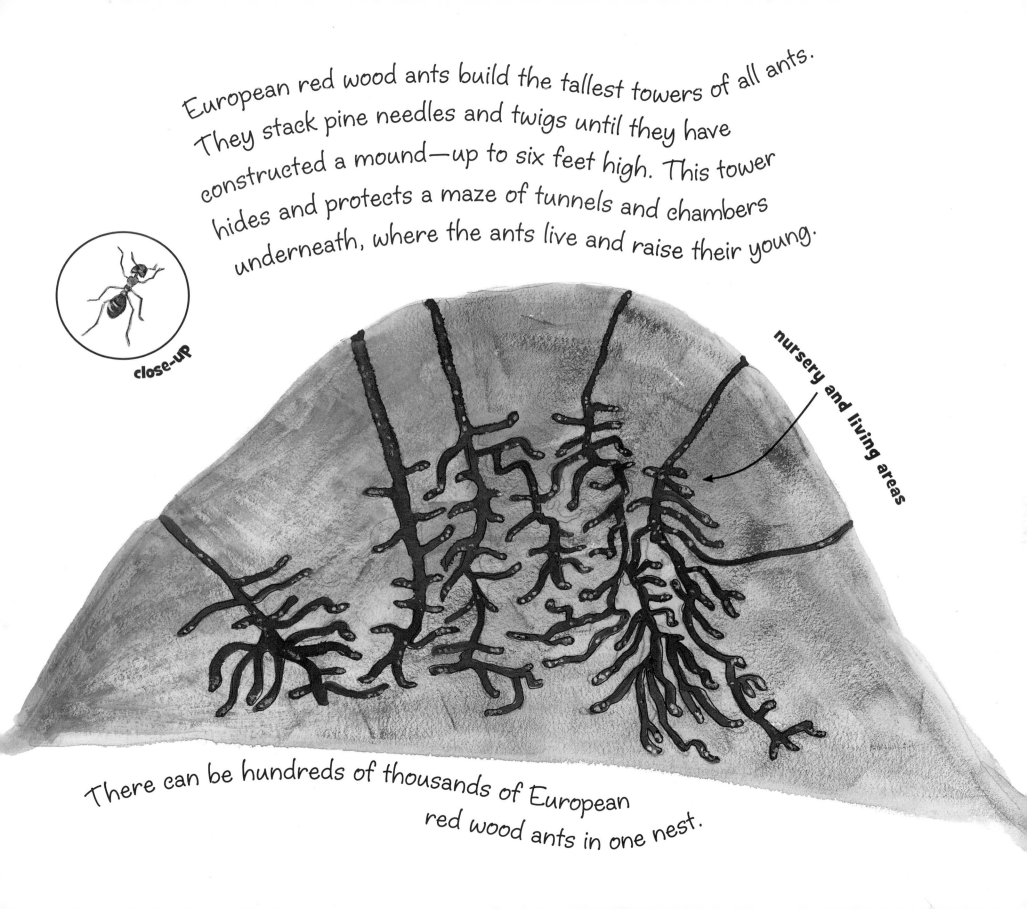

close-up

nursery and living areas

There can be hundreds of thousands of European red wood ants in one nest.

Towering homes are constructed underwater too. A single coral polyp is the size of a pencil eraser. By linking together and stacking on top of each other, the coral polyps create a colony on the ocean's floor called a reef.

sea fan coral

staghorn coral

brain coral

fan coral

hump coral

The Great Barrier Reef, off the coast of Australia, is made up of millions of coral polyps and spans more than twelve hundred miles. This reef has been growing for five hundred thousand years and is so gigantic that it can be seen from space! Reefs are like underwater cities—they are teeming with life.

About 1,500 species of fish live on the Great Barrier Reef. So do 4,000 types of mollusks and 30 different types of marine mammals.

cabbage leather coral

sea whip coral

lettuce coral

boulder coral

brain coral

fox coral

Lodges

Beavers are excellent carpenters. Their lodges can last twenty years! Before building their homes, beavers make a dam. Using their sharp front teeth, they cut down trees and chew them into logs. They create a dam by piling up the logs. The dam holds back the river water and causes a pond to form the perfect setting for the beaver lodge.

dam

To make their lodge, the beavers carefully stack logs and plaster them with mud. Then the beavers build a chimney to keep fresh air flowing into the lodge.

The beavers make two or more underwater tunnels:
one for everyday comings and goings and the others for emergency exits.
If a predator sneaks into one tunnel, the beavers can escape through another.

Caves

Our early human ancestors lived in caves, just like some animals.

A huge octopus lives in a tiny cave. How does it get in there? Easy—an octopus doesn't have any bones, so it can squeeze through a small opening. After a female octopus has found the perfect cave, she hangs about two hundred thousand eggs from the ceiling.

Moray eels squeeze into snug underwater caves too.

Brown bears need toasty homes where they can snooze away the winter. Some move into rock caves, some dig dens in the sides of mountains, and others curl up in hollow spaces under the roots of big trees.

Bear cubs are born in dens during the winter.

flying fox bats

Bats hang around all day long. They cling to the ceilings of caves with their talons, sleeping away the day. Mothers give birth upside down, and their new babies nurse upside down too. Caves are safe, hidden places for bats to raise their families.

close-up

Bracken Cave in Texas is home to a gigantic bat colony—
twenty *million* Mexican free-tail bats live there!
If you gathered all those bats together, they would weigh 270 tons—
that's heavier than forty-five elephants!

Many polar bears dig dens out of snowdrifts, and that's where they sleep during the coldest months. A pregnant polar bear usually creates two rooms in her den: one for herself and a nursery for her cubs.

The pregnant bear will give birth and raise her cubs tucked away in her sheltered home.

air vent

entrance tunnel

Ringed seals use sharp claws on their front flippers to carve out dens inside snowdrifts. They come and go through holes in the den's floors that lead to the frigid water below.

The seals give birth and tend to their pups inside these snug lairs.

Burrows

Some people build their homes underground. That way they stay cool in summer and warm in winter. Certain animals live underground too.

Badgers live in vast underground mansions. These burrows, or sets, can have more than a hundred entrances, fifty rooms, and a half mile of tunnels! Each set has shared living areas, private bathrooms, and bedrooms with soft beds of grass and straw.

Leaf-cutter ants tunnel deep into the earth to create an underground city where millions of ants can live. These ants carry leaves that are thirty times their weight to their nests. That's like a person carrying a pickup truck! The leaves are used as compost, or fertilizer, for a special type of fungus that the ants eat.

Rabbits live underground in cozy side-by-side burrows called warrens.

A pistol shrimp digs a burrow in a lagoon or reef. Sometimes the shrimp allows a goby fish to move into its home. Why? The shrimp has poor eyesight and needs to be warned when a predator is approaching.

The shrimp touches the tail of the goby fish with one antenna. When there is danger, the fish flicks its tail, and the two animals dart into the safety of their shared home.

A tortoise's strong shell is like armor. It protects the animal from hungry predators. When the tortoise is scared, it pulls its head, legs, and tail into its shell. But its shell isn't a home. Most tortoises live in habitats that are very hot or very cold.

They tunnel into the ground and make burrows where they are protected from the harsh weather.

A Couch's spadefoot toad has a shovel-shaped toe on its hind foot that's perfect for digging.

shovel-shaped toe

Floating homes

Some people make their homes on the water—in a houseboat.

Some birds live in floating homes too.

This canvasback duck hasn't spotted the egg a redhead duck deposited in her nest.

redhead duck

Many redhead ducks make their homes by collecting plants and shaping simple, floating nests in swamps. But some redhead ducks cheat. They lay their eggs in the nests of other ducks, letting them do all the work of hatching and raising the ducklings.

The male magpie goose constructs a nest by bending reeds and trampling them flat. Then he waits . . . for two females to come along! The females share the job of hatching the eggs and raising the goslings.

Mobile homes

When people want to take their homes on the road, they live in mobile homes. Many sea creatures live in movable homes too: seashells!

One of them is a little octopus called the paper nautilus, or argonaut.

argonaut inside shell

argonaut outside shell

The female uses the calcium she secretes to make a paper-thin shell where she will hide her delicate eggs. And sometimes when there's danger, she'll take shelter inside the floating nursery.

Hermit crabs don't make their own homes—they borrow the empty shells of other sea creatures. As a hermit crab grows, it moves into larger and larger shells. If the crab is lucky, a sea anemone will attach itself to its shell. By waving its stinging tentacles around, the anemone scares away predators.

anemone

When the weather is too dry, snails pull their soft bodies into their shells and seal themselves in with slime. They can stay in their shells with no food or water for months.

Bubbles

Some sailors live underwater in submarines. And one little spider makes its own underwater home . . . out of a single bubble.

spider inside bubble

The diving bell spider spins its silk into a ball, fills the ball with air, and drags it underwater. The bubble provides the spider with air to breathe and a place to lay its eggs and raise its spiderlings.

A male Siamese fighting fish builds a multibubble nest.

He gulps air and spits it out over and over again until he has created a bundle made up of hundreds of bubbles. After mating, he scoops the eggs into his mouth and spits them into the bubble ball to hide them.

There are many types of animal homes, ranging from deep underground burrows to towering mounds and from delicate bubbles to sturdy lodges. Some animals make homes that last a lifetime, while others make new homes every night. And some animals don't build homes at all; they simply move into caves or borrowed seashells.

But all animals, including humans, need homes for the same reason: to have a safe and snug place to live and raise a family.